HOW TO SUCCEED IN ACCOUNTING

TO: **Accounting Students**

FROM: **Irvin N. Gleim, Ph.D., CPA, CIA, CMA, CFM, CFII**

As a former accounting student and professor as well as the author of study guides for CPA, CMA, CIA, and EA certification, I have spent over 40 years developing an effective system to study for college-level and professional certification exams. This booklet was written because I wanted to share this system with **you**.

The Gleim system was developed to encourage you to think about learning and understanding in contrast to short-term memorization so you are properly prepared for your accounting career. **Your** future–upper-level classes, certification examinations, and your professional career–is our focus.

GLEIM® EXAM PREP

- You invested in your future by going to college after high school.
- You invested further by majoring in accounting, a profession that provides exceptional career opportunities.
- In spite of your success up to this point, your study methods are probably **not** as efficient as they could be. Many students experience false success based on short-term memorization.
- We are inviting and urging you to invest even further to improve the effectiveness of your study time by learning and understanding, **rather than** memorizing. This will help you earn better grades, pass your certification exam(s), obtain a degree, and become successfully employed.

You need professional competency to

1. Pass the CPA (Certified Public Accountant), CIA (Certified Internal Auditor), CMA (Certified Management Accountant), and/or EA (IRS Enrolled Agent) exams
2. Practice professional accounting
3. Work your way up to an executive position, own your own firm, and obtain professional success

Please read this booklet carefully to gain a competitive advantage over your peers. It contains all the information you need to begin your pursuit of a career in accounting.

HOW TO SUCCEED IN ACCOUNTING

HOW TO PREPARE FOR SUCCESS IN SCHOOL AND ON CERTIFICATION EXAMS

The central theme of this booklet is control: Establish plans, perform effectively, evaluate your performance, understand where you need improvement, and follow through with a solid strategy. This is an executive approach that will work for you, <u>especially if you aspire to be an executive</u>–and you should, because you will have the opportunity.

What is your objective? Presumably, it is to earn a degree in accounting and subsequently sit for the CPA, CIA, CMA, and/or EA exams.

Why? The prospects of employment are consistently expanding, and starting salaries remain high and stable. Certification can increase earning potential by up to 40%!

What then? What will you be doing in 5 years? 10 years? 15 years? No one knows for sure, but to the extent that you improve your study program and become a more qualified candidate, you will brighten your career prospects. You want to train not only to be a professional accountant but also to be ready for the opportunity for a successful career.

Planning Your Curriculum

1. Chronologically list all of your courses to date by semester (or quarter). Put credits and grades to the right.
2. Underneath this listing, organize a desirable schedule of remaining courses and credits.
3. Consult your university website, college and departmental requirements, and any other relevant materials.

   a. Make sure you will meet all the requirements to graduate.
   b. Have you planned your courses in the proper sequence in terms of prerequisites?
   c. Make sure you are completing the requirements to be eligible to take any relevant certification exams.

4. Review your schedule with an appropriate school advisor and confirm that it satisfies the requirements for your graduation. Don't guess. Use the university resources available to properly prepare your college curriculum.

Grades Are Important

Usually, a "B" average or higher is necessary to enter graduate programs and/or law school. Some CPA firms and other employers restrict their hiring to individuals with a "B" average or better. *

If your GPA is currently below an "A" average or if your previous academic successes involved more memorizing and less learning and application, then this booklet is particularly relevant to you. You must do your best in each course, especially those pertaining to your career. Other courses are also important because they affect your overall GPA and help make you a more well-rounded person. Your employer will be interested in you as a person, not just as an accounting technician.

. . . And So Are Student Activities

To their detriment, some students overemphasize grades. You also need to be well-rounded by developing your "people skills" and leadership abilities, which is harder to do now that many courses are taught online.

Join your accounting club or the honorary accounting fraternity, Beta Alpha Psi, if your school is a member of the American Association of Collegiate Schools of Business. To develop leadership skills, plan to serve as an officer. Create your own club. Volunteer to help low-income families with tax returns. Balance your academic efforts with other activities, such as community service, intramural sports, student government, or the pursuit of personal interests.

Almost all prospective employers are interested in your leadership, communication, **and** social skills. You will also need to be proficient in computer applications, so make sure to master those programs as well.

*If you currently are struggling with a "C" average, don't give up. These techniques should help you improve. While higher grades are preferred, many "C" or "C+" students are extremely successful once out of school.

Should You Go for a Master's Degree?

Just as your bachelor's degree is an investment in your future, so is a master's degree (MA, MS, or MBA).

Reasons to Pursue a Master's Degree

1. A master's in accounting provides you with even greater opportunities for employment and career advancement and translates to a premium salary. One study indicates as much as a 15% difference in yearly salary![1]

2. Your employer will have higher expectations as a result of your additional training. Usually this translates into better assignments, more responsibility, faster promotion, and higher compensation.

3. Positions for advanced employment frequently require (a) a master's degree; (b) the CPA, CMA, and/or CIA designation; and (c) several years of experience for accounting executive positions or managerial positions, such as controller or treasurer. Adding the EA designation will demonstrate your proficiency in tax matters.

4. Once you begin working long hours in a specialized field, resuming the role of a student is not easy. It's best to stay in school until your educational goals have been met, if possible.

Considering the Cost

Education is the best investment you will make! The amount and availability of financial support can be an impediment to continued education, but borrowing funds to pursue a higher level of education is generally a prudent financial decision, especially if you graduate with an accounting degree. A part-time job will also help defray some of your costs.

Delaying the Attainment of a Master's Degree

Many professionals attend graduate school on a part-time basis (evenings, weekends) if circumstances did not allow them to do so before entering the work force. These programs provide a chance to interact with peers who have similar interests and aspirations. An added benefit of attending graduate school part-time is learning from the work experience of classmates with various backgrounds, which significantly enriches class discussion. Your employer may also offer tuition assistance if the education furthers your employment with the company.

---

[1] Robert Half 2017 Salary Guide

The Basics of Learning and Understanding

Your Cognitive Processes

- Which mental processes do you use for learning?
- How do you internalize assignments?
- How do you process facts and concepts to complete assignments and take tests?

By better understanding how you study, you can learn to be more efficient and effective. If you improve your study processes by 20%, you can change 80% scores to 96% scores and reduce studying 30 hours per week to 24 hours. Let's learn how.

To Learn (According to Merriam-Webster Dictionary)

Main Entry: **learn**

Function: *verb*
Inflected Form(s): **learned**; **learn•ing**

transitive verb

1 a (1) **:** to gain knowledge or understanding of or skill in by study, instruction, or experience <*learn* a trade> (2) **:** memorize <*learn* the lines of a play>

b : to come to be able <*learn* to dance>

c : to come to realize <*learned* that honesty paid>

Psychologists have defined many categories of learning, such as **classical conditioning, trial-and-error learning, sensorimotor learning, verbal learning, concept learning, and rule learning**.

Accountants mainly focus on concept learning and rule learning. Most accounting and business concepts are multidimensional (i.e., relate to many concepts, rules, and relationships); therefore, they can be better understood by examining their multiple aspects. For example, you might view a financial accounting transaction in light of

1. Required journal entries
2. Impact on the financial statements
3. Consequences of the transaction for the business
4. Motivation of all parties to enter into the transaction
5. Behavioral implications to employees, customers, competitors, etc.

Train yourself to consider the contextual implications of the underlying business transactions for all accounting procedures you study. For example, what effect a given procedure or transaction will have on

- Purchasing power
- Financial ratios
- Cash flows
- Cost of capital
- Earnings per share
- Dividend growth

Levels of Cognitive Activity

One categorization of the levels of knowledge[1] can be illustrated by the following image:

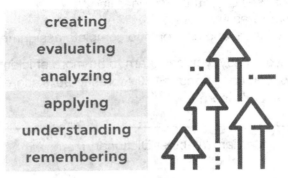

creating
evaluating
analyzing
applying
understanding
remembering

These levels are a revised version of Bloom's taxonomy[2], which has been used in curriculum planning, research, and other areas of education and psychology since 1956. The levels are cumulative—they constitute building blocks of cognitive processes. To understand something, you need to remember what you have already learned; to analyze problems, you must understand the concepts.

1. **Remembering.** Recalling knowledge, e.g., definitions of technical terms and sources of information. Objective questions often test this kind of knowledge, which is the most fundamental since it entails basic memorization. This requires little mental processing beyond simple recall.

    ACCOUNTING EXAMPLE: According to Statement on Financial Accounting Concepts (SFAC) No. 8, the two fundamental qualitative characteristics of accounting information are relevance and faithful representation.

2. **Understanding.** Understanding and interpreting written and quantitative data. Questions at this level test understanding of concepts, including interrelationships within data. This level of knowledge is also called comprehension.

    ACCOUNTING EXAMPLE: According to SFAC No. 8, "Relevant financial information is capable of making a difference in the decisions made by users. Financial information is capable of making a difference in decisions if it has predictive value, confirmatory value, or both." What does this mean? Do you understand? Can you explain it to someone else? The ability to explain a concept to someone else is an indicator of your comprehension.

3. **Applying.** Applying knowledge for problem solving. Questions at this level examine practical applications of concepts to solve a problem. Thus, applying combines both remembering and understanding in order to solve problems.

    ACCOUNTING EXAMPLE: Memorizing the cost of goods sold (COGS) formula is mere recall [COGS = BI (beginning inventory) + Pur (purchases) – EI (ending inventory)]. In order to solve more complex problems, such as the effect of inventory errors, you should also understand the relationship of the change in inventory level to COGS. For example, when EI is greater than BI, it means not all purchases were sold. Given BI, Pur, and EI, most students can solve for COGS simply by plugging numbers into the formula. But an interpretation of the relationship of the data is required for more complex problems.

---

[1] Anderson, L.W. and David R. Krathwohl, et al (Eds.,) (2001) A Taxonomy for Learning, Teaching, and Assessing: A Revision of Bloom's Taxonomy of Educational Objectives. Allyn & Bacon. Boston, MA (Pearson Education Group).

[2] Bloom, B.S. and David R. Krathwohl, (1956) Taxonomy of Educational Objectives: The Classification of Educational Goals, by a committee of college and university examiners. Handbook I: Cognitive Domain. NY, NY: Longmans, Green.

4.   **Analyzing.** Analytical ability, including identification of cause-and-effect relationships, internal consistencies or inconsistencies, relevant and irrelevant items, and underlying assumptions. The following question requires analysis and interrelation of a number of variables to reach a conclusion.

ACCOUNTING EXAMPLE: Would you accept a customer's order at a lower-than-usual price? Variables to consider include contribution margin generated, available production capacity, and psychological and economic effects on other customers.

5.   **Evaluating.** What is the best (most effective) method (alternative)? Evaluation, like analysis, takes into consideration qualitative as well as quantitative variables. Evaluation takes the process one step further, though; it involves making a judgment based on the results of the analysis.

ACCOUNTING EXAMPLE: The company received a special order to produce an additional 1,000 units. The decision to accept the special order requires evaluation of production capabilities and personnel availability.

6.   **Creating.** Designing, constructing, planning. In today's learning and business environments, students and professionals often create their own programs to suit their needs and goals. This type of activity involves the synthesis of multiple elements to either reform an existing structure or create an entirely new one.

ACCOUNTING EXAMPLE: A new company hires a consultant to analyze and evaluate its operations. The company wishes to have the consultant develop and design (create) a new system of internal controls that are better-suited to the company than those currently in place, which it has found to be inadequate.

Undergraduate accounting courses generally emphasize the first three levels of knowledge, while your career in professional accounting will require and emphasize the last three levels. Gleim products will help you reach these higher levels of thinking while preparing you for your exams.

Put another way, the first three levels of knowledge are required to prepare financial data. The second three levels are necessary to use financial data and exercise professional judgment. How does accounting differ from bookkeeping? Professional judgment.

In your study of accounting, you must go well beyond recall and memorization. Many accountants move on to executive positions after beginning their professional career as an "accountant." Even those who remain in accounting exercise more and more judgment and rely less and less on rote memory as they take on more responsibility and move upward in their career.

The Basics of Studying

Course Overview

At the very beginning of the term, as soon as you have your text and syllabus, create an executive overview of each course.

1. **Write down the chapter titles.** Using this information, ask yourself: What is the course about? How does its content relate to courses I have already taken and to courses I plan to take in the future?

2. **Skim each chapter.** Read the introduction and summary/conclusion. Your objective is to gain more insight into each chapter's content and approach than you gained from the chapter title analysis in 1. above.

3. **Document your effort.** Write a short paragraph and/or summary outline of each chapter.

4. **Examine the entire course overview.** Has your executive overview of the course changed and become more focused as a result of your analysis?

The entire process will probably take 2 to 4 hours. Spend half a day at the library and do a thorough job for each course. This initial investment of time will pay dividends because you have a basis for understanding how the chapters and their parts fit into the overall course at this point.

Now you will be able to put individual definitions and concepts into the context of the entire course. Through the exercise of control, you will be more efficient and effective and therefore better prepared to attain higher levels of knowledge.

Study Suggestions

Where to Study

Study where you study best. It's not one size fits all: Some study best at home, while others study best at the library. Some prefer to study at different locations at various times of the day and/or on different days. Still others study at only one location.

The issue is effective study. You must seek out the study locations that provide you with the most effective environment for concentration, which means avoiding or blocking out distractions most often produced by people you know. Try out-of-the-way places where other accounting majors and friends do not study, e.g., the law library. Consider turning off your cell phone.

When to Study

Study on a regular basis, 7 days a week to the extent possible. Stay ahead of all assigned material. Do **not** wait to study until just before exams and assignment due dates. Such a habit emphasizes rote memorization, which does **not** result in learning and understanding. You will improve your grade point average and increase the amount learned by investing several hours in each class at the very beginning of each term (as advised in "Course Overview" on the previous page).

Are you a morning person? Do you study more effectively in the morning or in the evening? Experiment with different study times to determine when you are most effective and schedule your time accordingly.

> A good rule to follow is, **"You are behind if you are not ahead."** You must **study regularly** to stay ahead. Class lectures and discussion are so much more meaningful and beneficial when you have studied the assignment **prior** to attending class.

How to Study a Chapter in a Textbook

Before reading a chapter, gain a general understanding of the chapter contents. The following seven steps should precede actual study:

1. **Read the chapter summary.** What is it about?
2. **Skim through the chapter.**
3. **Look at the requirements** of the exercises and problems to see what is expected.
4. **Try to answer the discussion questions** at the back of the chapter to see if you can provide answers based upon your present knowledge and common sense. If possible, relate real-life (business-world) examples to the discussion questions or requirements to help your understanding.
5. **Obtain and use** the appropriate Gleim **Exam Questions and Explanations** book and **EQE Test Prep** (detailed on page 15).

    Each Gleim product contains an extensive test bank of former exam questions and is thoroughly cross-referenced to textbooks used at universities throughout the U.S. Accordingly, you can identify specific areas in the Gleim book for each chapter in your textbook. Answer 5 to 10 questions to determine the standards to which you will be held. Gleim EQE Test Prep allows you to study, self-test, and measure your progress. Page 15 has more information.

6. **Outline the chapter** based on the headings. Rewrite them in your own words. **Do not** recopy phrases from the textbook. Put concepts into your own words so you understand and internalize rather than memorize them.
7. **Begin studying, rather than simply reading**. You now have an overview of the chapter and have thought about what is in it. Studying means understanding. What is the author saying? Do you agree? How does each concept fit into the chapter?

> Remember, the objective is **not** to read the chapter and complete an assignment. The objective **is to understand** the material well enough to be able to explain it to someone else. To this end, you need to be sufficiently conversant with the material in each chapter so that you can confidently discuss it, question it, and/or critique it with your professor, as well as assimilate it with class lectures and notes.

During Class Time

1. **Ask at least one question** during each class session. Engage your professor in discussion about a topic, procedure, or principle that you do not understand. Many beginning accounting students are introverts, sit passively in class, and only receive information. This approach is inefficient because these students simply write down formulas, definitions, etc., for later regurgitation without understanding the concepts.

2. **Stay ahead of your professor**, answer all questions asked (usually to yourself), and look ahead during lectures. Anticipate what will be next. Pre-class preparation permits you to learn in class. The poor alternative (both inefficient and ineffective) is to play "catch-up," i.e., attempt to memorize lists, definitions, etc., out of context after class is over. Remember, you have Gleim **Exam Questions and Explanations** products to supplement your study and significantly improve your preparation.

3. **Attempt to relate your current course material to that covered in previous courses.** A thorough understanding of the material in previous courses makes it feasible to tie the contents of all your courses together.

4. **Make notes in the margins of your books**; they are your study vehicle. Just as you should ask questions and discuss topics with your professor, you need to understand your text. Critique your text as you study! How could it be improved? How would **you** organize and present the material?

NOTE: Do **not** become completely dependent on highlighters and underlining! Yes, many students highlight and underline, but using short-term memory to become familiar with the concepts, facts, and definitions is only sufficient to complete courses. Remember that you are in school to learn and understand with the objective of a successful career, **not** just to get a diploma.

How to Complete Homework Assignments

Many accounting course assignments consist of computational problems that are largely similar to the examples and illustrations in your chapters. Thus, most of your homework problems are susceptible to "cookbooking," or copying from the chapter illustration, step-by-step. Barely more than rote memorization is required to achieve false success.

However, you will be adequately prepared to complete your homework assignments under **exam conditions** (time pressure and no reference back to the chapter) because you have previously accomplished the necessary building blocks in your individualized control process: establishing where and when to study, surveying the course, studying your textbook, answering multiple-choice questions in the Gleim **Exam Questions and Explanations** book and **EQE Test Prep**, and participating in class.

First, scan the exercise or problem and set a 5-, 10-, or 15-minute time limit. With a watch or clock handy, see how much you can accomplish within the time limit.

Next, as you get each problem under control, **note the issues you need to research** after you have substantially completed the problem.

Put yourself in a frame of mind to be **highly productive** during homework preparation. Effective time management is very important for successful exam performance. Do your best! No one can ask for more.

EFFICIENCY   TIME MANAGEMENT   PRODUCTIVITY

Develop and use your question-answering techniques on each homework assignment. These systematic methods of problem solving should be executive in nature. Before you start, determine what has to be done, how it has to be done, the sequence of procedures, etc. It is the same general **approach recommended for course overviews, studying a chapter, taking an exam, etc.**

How to Succeed on Exams – Preparation and Control

Preparation – In order to be successful on <u>academic</u> and <u>certification</u> examinations, you must

1. **Understand the exam, including coverage, content, format, administration, and grading.**

   For college courses: Ask your professor for clarification of the exam process publicly in class and privately in his or her office, talk to former students, and attempt to review exams from prior terms.

   For certifications: Virtually all certification programs (CPA, CIA, CMA, EA, etc.), admission tests, and other established exams have informational books developed by those responsible for the examination. For example, Gleim prepares and provides free to all customers and students comprehensive *Exam Guide* booklets that contain all of the information you need for complete understanding of the CPA, CIA, CMA, and EA exams. The better you understand the process, the better you will perform.

2. **Learn and understand the subject matter tested.**

   For college courses: Confirm text and chapter coverage with your professor. Also, to what extent are class lectures, examples, handouts, etc., tested?

   For certifications: Obtain content specification outlines for established exams. Confirm coverage by looking at past examinations (if available) and/or review manuals. For example, Gleim includes the content syllabus for each exam in the relevant Review book. That way, your assurance of coverage is right there!

3. **Practice answering recent exam questions to perfect your exam question-answering and time-management techniques.** Answering recent exam questions helps you understand the standards to which you will be held. It also helps you understand the material tested and gauge how you will need to manage your time to complete all questions.

   For college courses: See "How to Supplement Your Studies with Gleim Exam Questions and Explanations" on page 15.

   For certifications: Purchase the Gleim **CPA, CIA, CMA, and/or EA Review System** (www.gleimaccounting.com). Systems may include books, online Test Prep, Audio Lectures, online Review courses, Gleim Instruct video series, Study Planner, Essay or Simulation Bank, and access to a Personal Counselor. Gleim CPA and CIA now feature SmartAdapt™ technology, which guides candidates through a personalized learning path.

4. **Plan and practice exam execution.** Anticipate the exam environment and prepare a plan, including your arrival time, your manner of dress, the appropriate exam supplies, the expected number of questions and the format, the order in which you will answer questions, and the time you will spend on each question. Expect the unexpected and adjust!

   For college courses and certifications: Remember that your sole objective when taking an examination is to maximize your score. Most examinations are "curved," and you must outperform your peers.

5. **Most importantly, develop confidence and ensure success** with a controlled preparation program followed by confident execution during the examination.

Control – You must be in control to be successful during exam preparation and execution.

Control can also contribute greatly to your personal and other professional goals. Control is a process whereby you

1. Develop expectations, standards, budgets, and plans
2. Undertake activity, production, study, and learning
3. Measure the activity, production, output, and knowledge
4. Compare actual activity with expected or budgeted activity
5. Modify the activity, behavior, or production to better achieve the desired outcome
6. Revise expectations and standards in light of actual experience
7. Continue the process

The objective is to be confident that the best possible performance is being generated. Most accountants study and understand this process in relation to standard costs, i.e., establish cost standards and compute cost variances.

Every day you rely on control systems implicitly. Consider this simple example: When you get dressed, you have expectations about the desired appearance of your outfit and the time required to attain that appearance. You monitor your progress and make adjustments as appropriate, e.g., straighten your tie or iron your skirt.

Develop and enforce standards in all of your endeavors. Exercise control, implicitly or explicitly. Most endeavors will improve with explicit control. This is particularly true with certification examinations and other academic tests.

1. Practice your **question-answering and time-management techniques** (and develop control) as you prepare answers/solutions to practice questions/problems during your study program.

2. Develop explicit **control over your study programs** based on the control process discussed above.

3. Think about using **more explicit control systems** over any and all of your endeavors.

4. Seek **continuous improvement** to meet your needs given a particular situation or constraint. Additional practice will result in further efficiencies.

How to Supplement Your Studies with Gleim Exam Questions and Explanations

Experts on testing continue to view multiple-choice questions as a valid means of examining various levels of knowledge. Many of the questions on the **GMAT, GRE, LSAT,** and other entrance examinations are multiple-choice questions. Two major certification exams, the **EA and CIA,** remain 100% multiple-choice, and the percentage of multiple-choice and other forms of objective questions on the **CMA and CPA** exams remains very high.

Using objective questions to study for undergraduate examinations is an important tool not only for obtaining good grades but also for long-range preparation for certification and other examinations.

The following suggestions will help you study in conjunction with each Gleim **Exam Questions and Explanations** product:

1.   Locate the study unit that contains questions on the topic you are currently studying. The **Exam Questions and Explanations** Test Prep and books contain cross-references to the tables of contents of most textbooks.

2.   Work through a series of questions, selecting the answers you think are correct.

3.   **If you are using the Gleim book, do not consult the answer or answer explanations on the right side of each page until after you have chosen and written down an answer.**

   •   It is crucial that you cover the answer explanations and intellectually commit yourself to an answer. This method will help you understand the concept much better, even if you answered the question incorrectly. **EQE Test Prep** automates this process for you.

4.   Study the explanations to each question you answered incorrectly. In addition to learning and understanding the concept tested, analyze **why** you missed the question.

   Did you misread the question or misunderstand the requirement?
   Did you make a math error?
   Did you not know the concept tested?

Studying the important concepts that we provide in our answer explanations will help you understand the principles to the point that you can answer that question (and any others like it) successfully.

5.   Identify your weaknesses and take corrective action before you take a test. Prepare a summary analysis of your work on each subunit (topic). With **EQE Test Prep**, simply view your performance analysis information. The following are some sample column headings that you might use:

Date	Subunit	Time to Complete	Questions Answered	Avg. Time per Question	Questions Correct	Percent Correct

The analysis will show your weaknesses (areas needing more study) and also your strengths (areas of improvement). You can improve your performance on objective questions both by increasing your percentage of correct answers and by decreasing the time spent per question.

Improve Your Grades!

Use these objective question and explanation products to ensure your understanding of each topic you study in your accounting and business law courses. Access the largest bank of exam questions (including thousands from past certification exams) that is widely used by professors. Get immediate feedback on your study effort while you take your practice tests.

AUDITING & SYSTEMS EXAM QUESTIONS AND EXPLANATIONS
(Twenty-First Edition)

1. Engagement Responsibilities
2. Professional Responsibilities
3. Planning and Risk Assessment
4. Strategic Planning Issues
5. Internal Control Concepts and Information Technology
6. Internal Control – Sales-Receivables-Cash Receipts Cycle
7. Internal Control – Purchases, Payroll, and Other Cycles
8. Responses to Assessed Risks
9. Internal Control Communications and Reports
10. Evidence – Objectives and Nature
11. Evidence – The Sales-Receivables-Cash Cycle
12. Evidence – Purchases, Inventory, Payroll, and Other Cycles
13. Evidence – Key Considerations
14. Evidence – Sampling
15. Reports – Opinions and Disclaimers
16. Reports – Other Modifications
17. Related Reporting Topics
18. Preparation, Compilation, and Review Engagements
19. SSAEs – Examination, Review, and Agreed-Upon Procedures Engagements
20. Governmental Audits
21. Internal Auditing
22. Information Systems

COST/MANAGERIAL ACCOUNTING EXAM QUESTIONS AND EXPLANATIONS
(Twelfth Edition)

1. Overview and Terminology
2. Job Costing
3. Activity-Based Costing
4. Cost-Volume-Profit Analysis
5. Budgeting
6. Absorption vs. Variable Costing
7. Standard Costs and Variances
8. Nonroutine Decisions
9. Responsibility Accounting, Performance Measurement, and Transfer Pricing
10. Process Costing
11. Cost Allocation: Support Costs and Joint Costs
12. Quality
13. Capital Budgeting
14. Inventory Management: Traditional and Modern Approaches
15. Probability and Statistics
16. Regression Analysis
17. Linear Programming
18. Other Quantitative Approaches

FEDERAL TAX EXAM QUESTIONS AND EXPLANATIONS
(Twenty-Eighth Edition)

1. Gross Income
2. Exclusions from Gross Income
3. Business Expenses and Losses
4. Limitations on Losses
5. Other Deductions for Adjusted Gross Income
6. Deductions from AGI
7. Individual Tax Computations
8. Credits
9. Basis
10. Depreciation, Amortization, and Depletion
11. Capital Gains and Losses
12. Sale of Business Property
13. Nontaxable Property Transactions
14. Partnerships: Formation and Operation
15. Partnerships: Distributions, Sales, and Exchanges
16. Corporate Formations and Operations
17. Advanced Corporate Topics
18. Income Taxation of Estates, Trusts, and Tax-Exempt Organizations
19. Accounting Methods
20. Employment Taxes and Withholding
21. Wealth Transfer Taxes
22. Preparer Rules
23. Federal Tax Process and Procedure

FINANCIAL ACCOUNTING EXAM QUESTIONS AND EXPLANATIONS
(Twentieth Edition)

1. The Financial Reporting Environment
2. The Accounting Process
3. Reporting Income
4. The Time Value of Money
5. Current Assets, Cash, Accounts Receivable, and Notes Receivable
6. Inventories
7. Property, Plant, and Equipment
8. Depreciation and Depletion
9. Intangible Assets and Research and Development Costs
10. Investments
11. Current Liabilities, Compensated Absences, and Contingencies
12. Noncurrent Liabilities
13. Employee Benefits
14. Leases
15. Corporate Equity
16. Earnings Per Share
17. Accounting for Income Taxes
18. Accounting Changes and Error Corrections
19. Statement of Cash Flows
20. Financial Statement Disclosures
21. New Revenue Recognition Standard: Revenue from Contracts with Customers
22. Financial Statement Analysis
23. GAAP Accounting for Partnerships
24. Business Combinations and Consolidated Financial Reporting
25. Interim Financial Reporting
26. Foreign Currency Translation and Transactions
27. State and Local Governments
28. Not-for-Profit Entities

BUSINESS LAW/LEGAL STUDIES EXAM QUESTIONS AND EXPLANATIONS
(Eleventh Edition)

1. The American Legal System
2. The American Court System
3. Civil Litigation and Procedure
4. Constitutional Law and Business
5. Administrative Law
6. Criminal Law and Procedure
7. Tort Law
8. Contracts: The Agreement
9. Contracts: Consideration
10. Contracts: Capacity, Legality, Mutuality, and Statute of Frauds
11. Contracts: Parol Evidence, Conditions, Discharge, and Remedies
12. Contracts: Third-Party Rights and Duties
13. Sale of Goods: Contract Formation, Title, and Risk of Loss
14. Sale of Goods: Performance, Remedies, and Warranties
15. Negotiable Instruments: Types, Negotiation, and Holder in Due Course
16. Liability on Negotiable Instruments, Banking, and Documents
17. Secured Transactions
18. Suretyship
19. Bankruptcy Overview and Administration
20. Bankruptcy Liquidations, Reorganizations, and Adjustments
21. Personal Property and Bailments
22. Computers and the Law
23. Real Property: Interests and Rights
24. Real Property: Transactions
25. Mortgages
26. Creditor Law and Liens
27. Landlord and Tenant
28. Wills, Estate Administration, and Trusts
29. Agency
30. Partnerships and Other Entities
31. Corporations: Nature, Formation, and Financing
32. Corporations: Operations and Management
33. Federal Securities Regulation
34. Insurance
35. Environmental Law
36. Antitrust
37. Consumer Protection
38. Employment Regulation
39. International Business Law
40. Accountants' Legal Responsibilities

HOW TO SUCCEED IN ACCOUNTING

ACCOUNTING CERTIFICATION PROGRAMS

Overview

The **CPA (Certified Public Accountant)** Exam is the grandparent of all the professional accounting examinations. Its origin was in the 1896 public accounting legislation of New York. In 1917, the American Institute of CPAs (AICPA) began to prepare and grade a uniform CPA Exam. It is currently used to measure the technical competence of those applying to be licensed as CPAs in all 50 states, Guam, Puerto Rico, the Virgin Islands, the District of Columbia, and an ever-expanding list of international locations.

The **CIA (Certified Internal Auditor), CMA (Certified Management Accountant),** and **EA (IRS Enrolled Agent)** examinations are relatively new certification programs compared to the CPA. The CMA Exam was first administered in 1972 and the first CIA Exam in 1974. The EA Exam dates back to 1959.

Purpose

The primary purpose of professional exams is to measure the technical competence of candidates. Competence includes technical knowledge, the ability to apply such knowledge with good judgment, comprehension of professional responsibility, and ethical considerations. Additionally, the nature of these examinations (low pass rate, broad and rigorous coverage, etc.) has several important effects.

1. Candidates are forced to learn all of the material that should have been presented and learned in a good accounting program.
2. Relatedly, candidates must integrate the topics and concepts that are presented in individual courses in accounting education programs.
3. The content of each examination provides direction to accounting education programs; i.e., what is tested on the examinations will be taught to accounting students.

Should you become certified?

Certification is important to professional accountants because it provides

1. Participation in a recognized professional group
2. An improved professional training program arising out of the certification program
3. Recognition among peers for attaining the professional designation
4. An extra credential for the employment market/career ladder
5. A higher salary (CPAs can earn up to 15% more[1], CMAs can earn up to 28% more[2], and CIAs can earn up to 40% more than non-certified peers![3])
6. The personal satisfaction of attaining a recognized degree of competency

These reasons hold particularly true in the accounting field due to wide recognition of the CPA designation. Accountants and accounting students are often asked if they are CPAs when people learn they are accountants. Additionally, one or more designations is often required to obtain employment in the accounting field. Thus, there is considerable pressure for accountants to become *certified*.

Obtaining multiple certifications is important for the same reasons as initial certification. Accounting students and recent graduates should look ahead and obtain multiple certifications to broaden their career opportunities. The table of selected CIA, CMA, EA, and CPA examination data on the following page provides an overview of these accounting examinations.

---

[1] Robert Half 2017 Salary Guide
[2] Institute of Management Accountants' 2016 Salary Survey
[3] The Institute of Internal Auditors 2012 Internal Audit Compensation Study

Examination Content

The content of certification examinations is specified by the respective governing boards with lists of topics to be tested. In the Gleim CIA, CMA, EA, and CPA review materials, the content tested is divided into subtopics we call study units. A study unit is a more manageable undertaking than an overall part of each exam. The listings of study units on pages 19, 20, 21, and 22 provide an overview of the scope and content of these exams.

Examination Summary

	CPA (Certified Public Accountant)	CIA (Certified Internal Auditor)*	CMA (Certified Management Accountant)	EA (IRS Enrolled Agent)
Sponsoring Organization	American Institute of Certified Public Accountants	Institute of Internal Auditors	Institute of Certified Management Accountants	Internal Revenue Service
Contact Information	www.aicpa.org (888) 777-7077	www.theiia.org (407) 937-1111	www.imanet.org (800) 638-4427	www.irs.gov (313) 234-1280
Exam Parts	Auditing and Attestation (4 hrs.) / Business Environment and Concepts (4 hrs.) / Financial Accounting and Reporting (4 hrs.) / Regulation (4 hrs.)	1 – Essentials of Internal Auditing (2.5 hrs.) / 2 – Practice of Internal Auditing (2 hrs.) / 3 – Business Knowledge for Internal Auditing (2 hrs.)	1 – Financial Reporting, Planning, Performance, and Control (4 hrs.) / 2 – Financial Decision Making (4 hrs.)	1 – Individuals (3.5 hrs.) / 2 – Businesses (3.5 hrs.) / 3 – Representation, Practices, and Procedures (3.5 hrs.)
Exam Format	AUD: 72 multiple-choice questions 8 TBS / BEC: 62 multiple-choice questions 4 TBS 3 written communications / FAR: 66 multiple-choice questions 8 TBS / REG: 76 multiple-choice questions 8 TBS	Part 1: 125 multiple-choice questions / Parts 2 and 3: 100 multiple-choice questions	Parts 1 and 2: 100 multiple-choice questions 2 essays	Parts 1, 2, and 3: 100 multiple-choice questions
Avg. Pass Rate	AUD – 49% / BEC – 53% / FAR – 44% / REG – 47%	Pass rates are not yet available for the reorganized exam.	1 – 40% / 2 – 50%	1 – 61% / 2 – 64% / 3 – 86%
Testing Windows	January-March 10 / April-June 10 / July-September 10 / October-December 10	On demand throughout the year	January-February / May-June / September-October	May-February (e.g., 5/01/2018-2/28/2019)
Resources	gleimcpa.com	gleimcia.com	gleimcma.com	gleimea.com
Available Prep Course Student Discounts	Up to 20%	Up to 20%	Up to 20%	Up to 10%

*Reflects the information for the reorganized 2019 exam.

The CIA Exam

NOTE: The CIA Exam Syllabus is changing as of January 1, 2019. The study unit listing for the 2019 edition of Gleim CIA Review is not yet finalized at time of print. However, provided below are the domains from the revised CIA Exam Syllabus.

Part 1: Essentials of Internal Auditing
    I. Foundations of Internal Auditing (15%)
    II. Independence and Objectivity (15%)
    III. Proficiency and Due Professional Care (18%)
    IV. Quality Assurance and Improvement Program (7%)
    V. Governance, Risk Management, and Control (35%)
    VI. Fraud Risks (10%)

Part 2: Practice of Internal Auditing
    I. Managing the Internal Audit Activity (20%)
    II. Planning the Engagement (20%)
    III. Performing the Engagement (40%)
    IV. Communicating Engagement Results and Monitoring Progress (20%)

Part 3: Business Knowledge for Internal Auditing
    I. Business Acumen (35%)
    II. Information Security (25%)
    III. Information Technology (20%)
    IV. Financial Management (20%)

Visit our 2019 CIA Exam Changes info page at www.gleim.com/cia-exam-changes for more information about the revisions to the exam.

According to The IIA, the CIA is a "globally accepted certification for internal auditors" through which "individuals demonstrate their competency and professionalism in the internal auditing field." Successful candidates will have gained "educational experience, applicable knowledge, and business tools that can deliver a positive impact in any organization or business environment."

The CIA Exam is computerized to facilitate testing. Part 1 consists of 125 multiple-choice questions and lasts 2.5 hours, while Parts 2 and 3 each contain 100 multiple-choice questions and last 2 hours.

The first two parts of the CIA Exam focus on the theory and practice of internal auditing. The body of knowledge of internal auditing and the auditing skills to be tested consist of

1.   The typical undergraduate auditing class as represented by auditing texts

2.   Internal auditing textbooks

3.   Various IIA (Institute of Internal Auditors) pronouncements and Standards

4.   Reasoning ability, communications and problem-solving skills, and dealing with auditees in an audit context (i.e., the questions will cover audit topics but test audit skills)

Part 3 of the exam ensures that internal auditors are well-rounded and conversant with topics, methodologies, and techniques ranging from individual and organizational behavior to information security and technology.

Purchase Gleim CIA Review System with SmartAdapt - www.gleimcia.com

The CMA Exam

LISTING OF *CMA REVIEW* STUDY UNITS

Part 1: Financial Reporting, Planning, Performance, and Control

1. External Financial Statements and Revenue Recognition
2. Measurement, Valuation, and Disclosure: Investments and Short-Term Items
3. Measurement, Valuation, and Disclosure: Long-Term Items
4. Cost Management Concepts
5. Cost Accumulation Systems
6. Cost Allocation Techniques
7. Operational Efficiency and Business Process Performance
8. Analysis, Forecasting, and Strategy
9. Budgeting -- Concepts, Methodologies, and Preparation
10. Cost and Variance Measures
11. Responsibility Accounting and Performance Measures
12. Internal Controls -- Corporate Governance
13. Internal Controls -- Controls and Security Measures

Part 2: Financial Decision Making

1. Ethics, Fraud, and Risk Management
2. Financial Markets and Types of Securities
3. Valuation Methods and Cost of Capital
4. Managing Current Assets
5. Corporate Restructuring and International Finance
6. Ratio Analysis
7. Activity Measures and Financing
8. Investment Decisions
9. CVP Analysis
10. Marginal Analysis and Pricing

The CMA Exam consists of two parts: (1) Financial Reporting, Planning, Performance, and Control and (2) Financial Decision Making. Both parts consist of 100 multiple-choice questions and two 30-minute essay questions. A total of 4 hours is allowed for the completion of a part (3 hours for the multiple-choice, 1 hour for the essays).

According to the IMA, the "CMA is the advanced professional certification specifically designed to measure the accounting and financial management skills that drive business performance."

In their Resource Guide, the ICMA explains that through the certification test, "the requirements of the CMA Program . . . recognize those who can demonstrate that they possess a sufficient degree of knowledge and skills in the areas of management accounting and financial management. In this way, the ICMA helps identify practitioners who have met certain predetermined professional standards."

We have arranged the subject matter tested on the CMA Examination into manageable study units for each part. Each part is presented in a separate book. Both of these books contain review outlines; prior CMA Exam questions, answers, and answer explanations; and essay questions.

The CMA Exam has broader coverage than the CPA Exam in several areas. For example,

1. CMA topics like risk management, finance, and management are covered lightly, if at all, on the CPA Exam.
2. The CMA Exam focuses very heavily on internal decision making, such as special orders and capital budgeting, whereas the CPA Exam is concerned with external reporting.
3. The CMA Exam tests business ethics but not business law.

Also, CMA questions are generally more analysis-oriented than CPA questions.

Purchase Gleim CMA Review System - www.gleimcma.com

The EA Exam

LISTING OF *EA REVIEW* STUDY UNITS

Part 1: Individuals

1. Filing Requirements
2. Gross Income
3. Business Deductions
4. Above-the-Line Deductions and Losses
5. Itemized Deductions
6. Tax Credits, Other Taxes, and Payments
7. Basis
8. Adjustments to Asset Basis and Capital Gains and Losses
9. Business Property, Related Parties, and Installment Sales
10. Nonrecognition Property Transactions
11. Individual Retirement Accounts
12. Gift Tax
13. Estate Tax

Part 3: Representation, Practices, and Procedures

1. Practice before the IRS
2. Tax Preparers and Penalties
3. Representation
4. Examination of Returns and the Appeals Process
5. The Collection Process
6. Tax Authority
7. Recordkeeping and Electronic Filing

Part 2: Businesses

1. Entity Types, Methods, and Periods
2. Income, Farms, and Property Transactions
3. Business Expenses
4. Other Deductions
5. Basis
6. Depreciation
7. Credits, Losses, and Additional Taxes
8. Contributions to a Partnership
9. Partnership Operations
10. Disposition of a Partner's Interest
11. Corporations
12. Corporate Formation
13. Corporate Income and Losses
14. Corporate Deductions
15. Corporate Distributions
16. Corporate Liquidations and Redemptions
17. S Corporations
18. Decedent, Estate, and Trust Income Tax Returns
19. Retirement Plans for Small Businesses
20. Exempt Organizations

Enrolled agents are individuals who have demonstrated special competence in tax matters and professional ethics and have been enrolled to practice before the IRS as taxpayers' agents or legal representatives. Practice before the IRS includes all matters connected with presentations to the IRS relating to a client's rights, privileges, and liabilities under laws or regulations administered by the IRS. Such presentations include

1. Preparing and filing documents;
2. Communicating with the IRS; and
3. Representing a client at conferences, hearings, and meetings.

The examination covers federal taxation and tax accounting and the use of tax return forms for individuals, partnerships, corporations, trusts, estates, and gifts. It also covers ethical considerations and procedural requirements.

The exam consists of three parts, with 3.5 hours for each part (4 hours total seat time to include tutorial and survey). The questions on the examination are directed toward the tasks that enrolled agents must perform to complete and file forms and tax returns and to represent taxpayers before the Internal Revenue Service. Each part of the examination consists of 100 multiple-choice questions and covers the following tax topics:

Part 1 - Individuals
Part 2 - Businesses
Part 3 - Representation, Practices, and Procedures

Purchase Gleim EA Review System - www.gleimea.com

The CPA Exam

LISTING OF *CPA REVIEW* STUDY UNITS

Business
1. Corporate Governance Structure and Regulations
2. COSO Frameworks
3. Microeconomics
4. Macroeconomics
5. International Economics
6. Risk Return Principles
7. Financial Risk Management
8. Corporate Capital Structure
9. Working Capital I: Cash and Receivables
10. Working Capital II: Inventory and Short-Term Financing
11. Capital Budgeting
12. IT Roles, Systems, and Processing
13. IT Software, Data, and Contingency Planning
14. IT Networks and Electronic Commerce
15. IT Security and Controls
16. Performance Measurement and Process Management
17. Budget Components
18. Costing Fundamentals
19. Costing Methods
20. Costing Systems and Variance Analysis

Regulation
1. Ethics and Professional Responsibilities
2. Securities Law and Liability of CPAs
3. Federal Tax Authority, Procedures, and Individual Taxation
4. Accounting Methods and Gross Income
5. Self-Employment and Farming
6. Adjustments and Deductions from AGI
7. Credits, AMT, and Losses
8. Property Transactions
9. Corporate Taxable Income
10. Corporate Tax Computations
11. Corporate Tax Special Topics
12. S Corporations and Exempt Organizations
13. Partnerships
14. Estates, Trusts, and Wealth Transfer Taxes
15. Noncorporate Business Entities
16. Corporations
17. Contracts
18. Agency and Regulation
19. Sales and Secured Transactions
20. Debtor-Creditor Relationships

Auditing
1. Engagement Responsibilities
2. Professional Responsibilities
3. Planning and Risk Assessment
4. Strategic Planning Issues
5. Internal Control Concepts and Information Technology
6. Internal Control – Sales-Receivables-Cash Receipts Cycle
7. Internal Control – Purchases, Payroll, and Other Cycles
8. Responses to Assessed Risks
9. Internal Control Communications and Reports
10. Evidence – Objectives and Nature
11. Evidence – The Sales-Receivables-Cash Cycle
12. Evidence – The Purchases, Inventory, Payroll, and Other Cycles
13. Evidence – Key Considerations
14. Evidence – Sampling
15. Reports – Opinions and Disclaimers
16. Reports – Other Modifications
17. Related Reporting Topics
18. Preparation, Compilation, and Review Engagements
19. SSAEs – Examination, Review, and Agreed-Upon Procedures Engagements
20. Governmental Audits

Financial
1. The Financial Reporting Environment
2. Financial Statements
3. Income Statement Items
4. Financial Statement Disclosure
5. Cash and Investments
6. Receivables
7. Inventories
8. Property, Plant, Equipment, and Depletable Resources
9. Intangible Assets and Other Capitalization Issues
10. Payables and Taxes
11. Employee Benefits
12. Noncurrent Liabilities
13. Leases and Contingencies
14. Equity
15. Business Combinations and Consolidated Financial Reporting
16. Derivatives, Hedging, and Other Topics
17. Statement of Cash Flows
18. Governmental Accounting – Modified Accrual
19. Governmental Accounting – Full Accrual
20. Not-for-Profit Accounting and Reporting

The CPA Examination is designed to measure professional competence in auditing, business law, taxation, accounting, and related business topics, including

1. The command of adequate technical knowledge
2. The ability to apply such knowledge skillfully and with good judgment
3. An understanding of professional responsibilities

Passing this exam validates and confirms your professional accounting education and requires your complete dedication and determination. The benefits include higher salary, increased confidence and competence, and recognition as a member of an elite group of professionals.

The CPA Exam is administered the first 2 months and 10 days of every calendar quarter (i.e., January 1 - March 10, April 1 - June 10, July 1 - September 10, and October 1 - December 10) at Prometric testing centers throughout the U.S. and at select international locations. The exam is divided into four sections: Auditing and Attestation (AUD), Business Environment and Concepts (BEC), Financial Accounting and Reporting (FAR), and Regulation (REG). Each section consists of a series of testlets.

Each CPA Exam section is divided into five testlets. Each testlet is dedicated to a specific type of CPA Exam question.

Types of Questions:

- **Multiple-choice questions** appear in the first 2 testlets and account for 50% of the total score in all four sections. The number of MCQs varies by section: AUD has 72, BEC has 62, FAR has 66, and REG has 76.
- **Task-Based Simulations** account for 50% of the total score in AUD, FAR, and REG, and 35% in BEC. AUD, FAR, and REG each have 8 TBSs total, while BEC has 4.
- **Written Communication Tasks** only appear in BEC and account for the final 15% of the total score. There are 3 WCs in BEC.

Steps to Passing Certification Exams

1. Become knowledgeable about the exam you will be taking, and determine which part you will take first.
2. Purchase the complete Gleim Review System to thoroughly prepare yourself. Commit to systematic preparation for the exam as described in our review materials.
3. Communicate with your Personal Counselor to design a study plan that meets your needs. Call (800) 874-5346 ext. 498 or email personalcounselor@gleim.com.
4. Apply for membership in the exam's governing body and/or in the certification program as required.
5. Register online to take the desired part of the exam.
6. Schedule your test with the testing center in the location of your choice.
7. Work systematically through each study unit in the Gleim Review System.
8. Sit for and PASS the exam while you are in control. Gleim guarantees success!
9. Email or call Gleim with your comments on our study materials and how well they prepared you for the exam.

What's Next??

Enjoy your career, pursue multiple certifications (CIA, CPA, EA, CMA, etc.), and recommend Gleim to others who are also taking these exams. Once you are certified, stay up-to-date on your Continuing Professional Education requirements with Gleim CPE.